WHAT
WHERE
WHY ?

What Makes Weather?

by Helen Orme

Gareth Stevens Publishing
A WORLD ALMANAC EDUCATION GROUP COMPANY

Please visit our web site at: www.garethstevens.com
For a free color catalog describing Gareth Stevens Publishing's list of
high-quality books and multimedia programs, call 1-800-542-2595 (USA)
or 1-800-387-3178 (Canada). Gareth Stevens Publishing's fax: (414) 332-3567.

Library of Congress Cataloging-in-Publication Data

Orme, Helen.
    What makes weather? / by Helen Orme.
      p. cm. — (What? Where? Why?)
    Includes index.
    Contents: What makes weather? — What are clouds made of? — Why does it rain? —
What are rainbows made of? — What are hail and snow made of? — What makes wind? —
How strong can wind blow? — What causes thunder and lightning?
    ISBN 0-8368-3788-6 (lib. bdg.)
    1. Weather—Juvenile literature. [1. Weather.] I. Title. II. Series.
QC981.3.O76   2003
551.6—dc21   2003045716

This North American edition first published in 2004 by
Gareth Stevens Publishing
A World Almanac Education Group Company
330 West Olive Street, Suite 100
Milwaukee, Wisconsin 53212 USA

Original copyright © 2003 by ticktock Entertainment Ltd. First published in Great Britain in 2003
by ticktock Media Ltd., Unit 2, Orchard Business Centre, North Farm Road, Tunbridge Wells,
Kent, TN2 3XF, England. This U.S. edition copyright © 2004 by Gareth Stevens, Inc.

Gareth Stevens series editor: Dorothy L. Gibbs
Gareth Stevens cover design: Melissa Valuch

Picture Credits
[Abbreviations: (t) top, (b) bottom, (c) center, (l) left, (r) right]
Alamy Images: pages 1(tr), 2(bl), 4(tl, tc, bl), 6(tl), 8(cl, br), 9(bl, tr), 10(bl, br), 11(bl), 16(tl, bl, br),
18(tl), 19(t), 20(tl), 22(tl), 24(tr).
Corbis: front cover, pages 2(tl), 10(tl), 15(tr), 18(cl), 21(cr).
NASA: pages 4(tr), 6(cr).

Every effort has been made to trace the copyright holders for the pictures used in this book.
We apologize in advance for any unintentional omissions and would be pleased to insert the
appropriate acknowledgements in any subsequent edition.

With thanks to: Lorna Cowan; Steven Dorling at the University of East Anglia, Norwich, England;
and Elizabeth Wiggans.

Printed in Hong Kong

1 2 3 4 5 6 7 8 9 07 06 05 04 03

CONTENTS

Words in the glossary are printed in **boldface** type the first time they appear in the text.

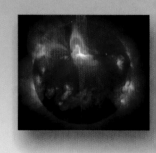

Take a look out the window. Weather is all around. What is the weather like today?

a cloudy day

a sunny day

a rainy day

On some days, the weather is sunny when you wake up but rainy after breakfast, when you want to go outside to play. Sometimes the weather makes you feel hot, and sometimes it makes you feel cold.

Have you ever wondered why weather changes? Have you ever wondered what causes thunder or what rainbows are made of?

a snowy day

What makes weather?

Lots of things make weather the way it is, but the Sun is the most important thing.

The Sun is a giant ball of burning **gas**.

The Sun makes heat and light, warming up our **planet**, making perfect conditions for life.

Is the Sun smaller or bigger than Earth?
(answer on page 23)

Without the Sun, we would not have sunshine!

The Sun heats up some parts of Earth more than others.

A desert is one of the warmest places on Earth.

North Pole (Arctic)

equator

South Pole (Antarctica)

The land and sea near the middle of Earth, at the **equator**, are hotter than the land and sea at each of Earth's **poles**.

Antarctica is one of the coldest places on Earth.

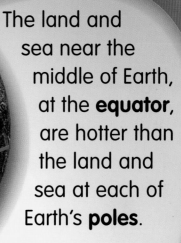

The warmer air and ocean **currents** at the equator move from the hottest places toward the coldest places.

This movement makes different types of weather.

What are clouds made of?

a) dust

b) water

c) snow

(Turn the page to find out.)

What are clouds made of?

Clouds look **solid**, but they are actually made of millions of tiny drops of water and **ice crystals**.

These drops and crystals are so small they float in the air.

Clouds with sharp edges are made of water **droplets**. Clouds with fuzzy edges are made of ice crystals.

Clouds that are low and near the ground are called **fog**.

Weather changes all the time.
You might wake up in bright sunshine. . .

What do cirrus, cumulus, and stratus clouds look like?
(answer on page 23)

. . .but after breakfast, the sunshine could be gone.

By then, clouds might have covered the Sun.

The weather might even be rainy!

Why does it rain?

a) *because the air gets too hot*

b) *because clouds get too heavy*

c) *because the air gets too cold*

(Turn the page to find out.)

Why does it rain?

Clouds bring rain.

The tiny drops of water in clouds join together, making bigger drops.

When the drops of water get too big, they are too heavy to float in the air.

Then, the drops fall as rain.

People wear special clothes when it rains so they will not get wet.

In some countries, almost all rain falls at a time of the year called the **monsoon** season.

monsoon flood

Where does the rain go after it falls?
(answer on page 23)

Monsoon rains are very heavy and last for hours. After this rainy season, the weather is very dry for the rest of the year.

Some places, such as a desert, have very little rain at any time of the year.

How often does it rain where you live?

What are rainbows made of?

a) water

b) hail

c) colored light

(Turn the page to find out.)

What are rainbows made of?

Rainbows are made of colored light.

They appear when the Sun comes out after a rainfall, and tiny water drops are still floating in the air.

The colors of a rainbow always appear in the same order: red, orange, yellow, green, blue, **indigo**, and violet.

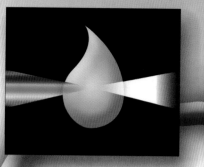

When sunlight shines through a raindrop, it comes out looking like bands of colored light. The colored light forms a rainbow.

You will never find the end of a rainbow.

What happens when you see two rainbows together?
(answer on page 23)

As you move, the rainbow also seems to move, at the same rate.

You can make your own rainbow by holding a **CD** in sunlight. A shiny CD splits **rays of light** into bands of color the same way a drop of water does.

What are hail and snow made of?

a) ice crystals

b) sunlight

c) lightning

(Turn the page to find out.)

What are hail and snow made of?

ice crystals

Some raindrops start as ice crystals. As they fall into warmer air, most of the **frozen** drops **melt** into rain.

If the ice crystals are too big, they will not melt. Then we have **hail** instead of rain. Sometimes, the hailstones are very large.

How can snow cause sunburn?
(answer on page 23)

Winter air is often so cold that even smaller ice crystals will not melt. The crystals stick together, making **snow**.

If the ground is as cold as the air, the snow will pile up on it.

All snowflakes have six sides, but no two snowflakes look alike.

scarf

hat

gloves

When snow falls for a long time, the piles can get very deep. Then it's time for fun. But dress warmly!

What makes wind?

a) electricity

b) moving air

c) thunderstorms

(Turn the page to find out.)

What makes wind?

Wind is air moving from one place to another.

Wind blows the leaves off of trees and makes their branches move around.

Wind also moves the clouds along in the sky.

Although you cannot see wind, you can see what it does.

Wind can be very useful. **Windmills** use wind to make power.

Some windmills use the power they make to grind grain into flour. The flour is used to make bread.

What do we use to measure wind direction? (answer on page 23)

Today, we have **wind farms**, where wind turns the blades on many rows of windmills to make electricity.

Wind is useful in sports, too! Windsurfers need it to ride the waves.

What is the name of a very strong windstorm?

a) breeze

b) mist

c) hurricane

(Turn the page to find out.)

17

How strong can wind blow?

Sometimes, wind blows so strong it can be frightening.

Trees often lose their branches in autumn **gales**. Stronger winds do even more damage.

Hurricanes are very strong windstorms. These storms start over the ocean and can travel great distances.

When they reach land, they do a lot of damage.

Hurricanes can blow cars into the air, rip the roofs off houses, and pull trees out of the ground.

How fast can wind blow?

(answer on page 23)

A **tornado** is another strong windstorm. It is a spinning **column** of wind that looks like a **funnel** of dark clouds reaching into the sky.

A tornado moves very quickly, destroying almost everything in its path.

What causes thunder and lightning?

a) wind

b) electricity

c) mist and fog

(Turn the page to find out.)

19

What causes thunder and lightning?

Especially in summer, when the air gets very hot, storm clouds produce electricity.

We see the electricity as flashes of lightning.

A **lightning bolt** strikes the highest object it finds, whether the object is a tree, a building, or a person. Lightning strikes can cause a lot of damage.

When a storm happens at night, the lightning is bright enough to see by.

a tree that was struck by lightning

Electricity causes **thunder**, too. Lightning moves quickly, making the air around it very hot — very fast!

Why does lightning always come before thunder?
(answer on page 23)

Thunder is the loud noise air makes when lightning heats it up.

Most thunderstorms bring heavy rainfall.

But thunderstorms can also be dry. The raindrops dry up before they reach the ground.

GLOSSARY

CD: compact disc.

clouds: masses of tiny drops of water or bits of ice floating in the air, usually high overhead.

column: a tall, thick post or pole, or something that looks like one.

currents: the movements or flow of water, especially in a large body of water.

droplets: very small drops.

equator: an imaginary line around Earth, halfway between the North and South Poles. It marks the region that receives the greatest amount of direct sunlight throughout the year.

fog: clouds that settle on or near the ground, making it difficult to see objects that are not very close.

frozen: turned into ice, usually as a reaction to cold temperatures.

funnel: a cone-shaped utensil with an opening at the bottom, used to pour liquid from a large container into a smaller one.

gales: strong winds, blowing at speeds of 32 to 63 miles (51 to 101 kilometers) per hour.

gas: a colorless and odorless substance that is not a solid or a liquid and will expand to fill any open space.

hail: small balls of frozen rain that fall to the ground, usually during a thunderstorm.

hurricanes: powerful storms with winds blowing more than 75 miles (120 km) per hour.

ice crystals: frozen water droplets that have a snowflake-like pattern.

indigo: a dark, bluish purple color, named after a dye that comes from the indigo plant.

lightning bolt: a single flash of light in the sky, produced by electricity inside a cloud.

melt: to turn into a liquid, usually as a reaction to warm or hot temperatures.

monsoon: a wind over the area around the Indian Ocean, which changes direction with the seasons, bringing frequent, heavy rain when it is blowing from the southwest and dry air when it is blowing from the northeast.

planet: a large ball made of rock or gas, or a combination of rock and gas, that travels in space, around the Sun.

poles: the places on Earth that are the furthest away from the equator, both to the north and to the south. The North Pole and the South Pole get the least amount of direct sunlight throughout the year.

rays of light: thin beams of light moving in a straight line.

snow: ice crystals that fall to Earth.

solid: having a defined shape and can be touched or held.

thunder: the rumbling sound heard after flashes of lightning.

tornado: a violent, whirling windstorm in a funnel-shaped cloud that moves along a narrow path over the ground.

wind farms: areas of land with rows of windmills that produce electricity.

windmills: buildings with armlike blades that turn in the wind, creating power or energy.

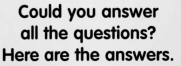

Could you answer all the questions? Here are the answers.

page 6: The Sun is much bigger than Earth.

page 9: Cirrus clouds are wispy. Cumulus clouds are puffy. Stratus clouds are flat.

page 11: Some rain goes into rivers, some into the ground, and some down storm sewers.

page 13: When two rainbows appear together, the colors in one rainbow are in the reverse order, which is violet, indigo, blue, green, yellow, orange, and red.

page 14: Snow reflects sunlight, and reflected light can burn your skin as easily as direct sunlight.

page 17: Weather vanes measure wind direction.

page 19: In 1999, a tornado roared through Oklahoma at speeds of up to 318 miles (512 kilometers) per hour!

page 21: Light travels much faster than sound.

23

INDEX